Additional Praise for *Red Rain*

Edytta Wojnar's *Red Rain* is superbly crafted and utterly original. It's not just a chapbook of powerful vignettes…it's a manifesto on power from a woman refusing the violences and silences thrust upon her. With an unflinching gaze, Wojnar chronicles childhood rape, marital betrayal, and how it affects how she moves through the world. At the same time, she lifts up her hopes of what will be different for her daughter in moments of vivid beauty and tenderness. This is a book from a poet who believes there's still time for a different story for women, including herself.
—Emily Sernaker

A series of violations haunts *Red Rain*: A childhood rape, the woman's concern for her own violated daughter, the Covid pandemic which forces people into isolation and fear as well as entrapment with their intimate partners. How revealing, yet surprising, are the poet's metaphors as these about her husband: "your body / a crossbow / a rainbow—i can't decide," Is it a weapon, dangerous, or a rainbow, insubstantial but visible, beautiful, promising? Finally, the tension between her and her husband culminates when she finds "a single zirconia / stud you won't recognize…/ waiting between the sheets." But there is a toughness here, as when in "Me too" she promises her daughter, "you will be unbreakable." What keeps the poet afloat is faith, not religious faith, but faith in the small miracles of the world and in her own pursuit of language strong and agile enough to encompass these experiences. With "bluebirds [which] bring a message / of hope," even though one "mistook glass for air // my home for heaven." Like Emily Dickinson, Wojnar "dwell[s]in possibility," sometimes ambiguous, tentative, but often daring.
—Mary Makofske, author of *No Angels*

Red Rain

poems by

Edytta Wojnar

Finishing Line Press
Georgetown, Kentucky

Red Rain

Copyright © 2025 by Edytta Wojnar
ISBN 979-8-89990-249-9 First Edition
All rights reserved under International and Pan-American Copyright Conventions. No part of this book may be reproduced in any manner whatsoever without written permission from the publisher, except in the case of brief quotations embodied in critical articles and reviews.

ACKNOWLEDGMENTS

Grateful acknowledgment is made to the editors of the following publications where some of the poems in this book, sometimes in a different form, first appeared:

Lips: "Lonesomeness," "Me too," "Neighbor"
NarrativeNortheast: "the third rock," "the god particle"
Persephone's Daughters: "Give-&-Take"
Ponder Review: "Half Snake Half Bird"
The Paddock Review: "Between 3 am & Dusk"
The Stillwater Review: "i can't decide," "We go on"
SurVision Magazine: "Mirage"
Waxing & Waning: "The Year of COVID" revised as "Remote Control"

Publisher: Leah Huete de Maines
Editor: Christen Kincaid
Cover Art: *Women in Society* by Karina Wojnar Schiesel
Author Photo: Gerard Byrne
Cover Design: Sebastian Wojnar

Order online: www.finishinglinepress.com
also available on amazon.com

Author inquiries and mail orders:
Finishing Line Press
PO Box 1626
Georgetown, Kentucky 40324
USA

Contents

Red Rain 1

the third rock 2

Half Snake Half Bird 3

Miscarriage 4

Exposure 5

Me too 6

Testimony 7

The Shape of Sleeplessness 8

Give-&-Take 9

No Words 10

i can't decide 11

Going out on a Cold Night 12

Lonesomeness 13

Neighbor 14

Between 3 am & Dusk 15

Remote Control 16

I Miss Mask Mandates 18

Inertia 19

Mirage 20

the god particle 21

We go on 22

With Gratitude 23

*For my daughter, Karina
my mom, Ludmiła
sisters, Monika & Milena
cousin, Martyna
& nieces, Anya & Emilka—
with love*

What matters in life is not what happens to you but what you remember and how you remember it.

~ Gabriel García Márquez

Being a poet sometimes puts you at the mercy of life, and life is not always merciful.

~ James Wright

Red Rain

Sleet. Hail. Snow.   Golf balls
once played into the sea   whirled by the wind.
A cow caught in a twister. Cats & dogs.
Frogs.   Lluvia de peces when fish
are carried inland by a tornado.

Somewhere frozen iguanas fall. Spiders.
      Space junk.   Money.

Years ago I fell for a boy.

Night falls on the lake
like a black wrinkled veil   & I fall
on shards of glass   at a neighborhood picnic.

When I was a child
I fell a victim to a pedophile—
      a velvet ribbon with the house key
      & his hands   on my neck—
"Staying Alive" on the radio
to muffle all sounds.   Drapes drawn.

Somewhere blood falls.

the third rock

from somewhere up
looks like an abstract work of art—

splashes of blue pacific waters
& blurred lands smeared by cirrus.

when one stays there for a while
even the grass blades threaten.

mountains spew volcanic ash
soil trembles & traps

wheels spin upside down
with bodies still buckled in.

somewhere in midday light a girl is
raped —a saffron flower in her hair.

meanwhile little fingers
count dots on ladybugs

sweet mango juice smears the chins
red-bellied robins rise from forsythia flames

swans' long necks bend
with tenderness towards each other

& lovers fall asleep easily—
a new life forming

under the wisps of clouds.

Half Snake Half Bird

Through the kitchen window, I see her tanned body sprawled in a lounge chair by the lake, her sunhat brighter than the pink Dahlias blooming in a flower bed by the patio. I stop rinsing berries when my phone lights up with a message. *There is a snake in the water,* she texts & adds an emoji of anguish to the photo she snapped. A snakehead with a sharp beak, droplets of water on its slim neck, appears on my iPhone. *It has wings! It's freaky!!!* Exclamation marks pulsate in my palm. *I've seen it before,* I text back, *it's a snakebird.* A confused smiley lights the screen followed by her message: *Wikipedia says your snakebird is an anhinga.* Instead of slicing mozzarella for Caprese, I google anhinga & watch a kettle of birds with long rubbery necks wheel on my six-inch screen while on the stove a kettle whistles warning. "The kettling of anhingas is an announcement of imminent departure," I read & look out the window again. I fill two glasses with Pellegrino & drop in a handful of raspberries. By the time I reach the bottom of the stone steps by the shore, the drinks fizz scarlet.

When I plop down into a low chair next to my daughter, water spills staining red the white shorts I am wearing. I sigh & laugh at my clumsiness. She sits up & laughs, too. "I remember the summer night you were born," I say. She stops laughing & stares at the horizon where the sky bleeds a palette of reds & a gibbous moon starts to swell. She sets her glass on the table, flings her sunhat on the grass. Rounding her back, she curls up on my lap. The strands of her wild purple hair she dyed in her dorm before visiting home tickle my cheek. "I smell lemongrass," I say, caressing her warm, bare shoulders, droplets of sweat pooling on her skin like morning dew. She says she skipped her period, twice, but doesn't want to talk about it now. She pulls my arms tighter around her waist. In the lake, a snakelike neck emerges, & a pair of wings slaps water. "I love you," I whisper in her ear. When a mosquito lands on her hip, I smack it. She jolts & looks up startled. I show her my palm with a trace of blood, & we gaze in silence at the tiny remains.

Miscarriage

a mortal cycle
of a moon that wanes
back into a sliver
or
cells like grapes
clots of blood soaking a pad
& you bent in half

Exposure

I don't remember the cause of my abdominal pain
the test's results or doctor's opinion

yet every time I have to lie on an x-ray table
I recall my freshman year being asked

to remove all clothing except my underwear
lie on my back on a starched white sheet

hold completely still while
the machine guided by a technician's hand

focuses on my concave stomach & as instructed
I hold my breath while his fingers

like invisible beams slip beneath my panties
parting my thighs

his penetrating eyes lock with mine before he slides
behind a glass fence
     a smirk on his face.

Me too

you sigh & tweet
#Metoo. Mothers nod
used to silence.

I will tell you one thing:

Nights reel darkness,
but each morning unfurls a new
radiant blossom.

The soft spot
below your solar plexus
will harden with confidence.

You will be unbreakable.

One day, your brothers,
boyfriends, & bosses
will be unbroken, too.

Caring. Most men are
not Weinstein, a coach
or a parish priest.

When you have a son—
be loving. But now
speak!

Testimony

       thunderous thoughts gallop
       through the nights   questions
       like hooves   leaving bruises

consider a 13-year-old
on her way from school   a key on a ribbon
lightly swaying & tapping the buttons
of her navy-blue uniform

consider Virgin Mary
a ruby crown on her child's forehead
in a monastery   commemorated
with a deep double-slash on her right cheek

how she's looking down   on the girl
who after the rape   went on a pilgrimage
to Częstochowa to cherish the Black Madonna

consider the girl   confessing
to a man hidden behind a screen
her sins   he would not absolve

consider her at 33   married   asleep

then a woman at 53   recalling men
lined up behind a one-way mirror
asking her mother if the one   who hurt her
was ever imprisoned

her mom not knowing   cries
how dreadful police
examination made her feel
her daughter   describing the facts

nobody had ever asked
the girl   how she felt

The Shape of Sleeplessness

heat rattles walls where rodents
perform the *danse*
       macabre   on a forearm
the pen's nib retraces
each letter until the blue ink
turns red
       upstairs a door squeaks

what time is it?

ink in her veins flattens
her bones   sheets wrinkle the skin
nonsense words slip
drip   water drips
           circling thoughts
                    against
time that writhes hands

Give-&-Take

The moonflower blooms
in darkness, its fragrance a promise
that things get better.

You give me sunflowers & hope
to have sex. It's prostitution, I say.

It's different in marriage.
It's not about sex, you protest,
even though it is. Most of the time.

Blades of grass hold the footprints.
Morning glories linger.

No Words

There are no names for the sweetness that swells
at the roots of nerves

wisps of touch
coiled on salty skin.

There are no notes that transcribe the round cries
curled around collarbones

the song muffled
by lips pressed to lips.

There are no words to describe the moment
when bodies strip reason & eyes lock.

i can't decide

the lake is a mirror—
a gateway to reveries—your body

a rainbow
a crossbow—i can't decide

the alarm goes off
& fog descends on black ice—

the morning is wrinkled & lights
dimmed—we sip coffee

in silence
a door thuds behind you—

snow crystals crack
& the sun hesitates

Going out on a Cold Night

You want to know the specials
& spices in Pappardelle Pescatore—

the vowels in your mouth round
the p's popping r's rolling seductively

you ask for the names of drafts
& which bottled beer she would recommend.

You like to try a different one
each time you go out—

the young waitress smiles
twirls wisps of blond hair with her pen

& leans in to take your order. I am not hungry.
I ask for a glass of Merlot.

You say for once you want to have
a meal & enjoy it. Sipping your amber ale

you stare when I say that just once
I wish to stay in the spotlight.

Lonesomeness

Silence hangs. I use silence

as line breaks

in my ritual of rainmaking.

Words fill cracks

in the eroding space—my husband

pulls weeds watching

a neighbor who builds

a stonewall by his porch

late into the night every night

his new girlfriend in front

of a blue screen that blinks

like a lighthouse.

Neighbor

Seeing her glamorous smile
one wouldn't think school
shootings keep her up at night.
One wouldn't suspect she dreams
of flying to Nepal to climb
the Himalayas or that she's addicted
to the feeling of
suffering & Dostoyevsky.

Seeing her smile softens
the edge you find yourself on
too often to your liking
& you are surprised to admit
you like her.

Seeing her smiling at you
you don't suspect she despises
babysitting your children
when you are working late.
You don't suspect her naked
body in your silk robe,
her fingers gently feeling
the lace of every bra in your drawer,
your perfume concealing
her scent in your bed.

Seeing her smiling for the photo
your husband is taking with his iPhone
in your garden—her back arched
against the sapless trunk of a pine,
pink shorts, hands in the pockets,
you are smiling too—a single zirconia
stud you won't recognize at night
waiting between the sheets.

Between 3 am & Dusk

The thought of not being
steals my breath at 3 am

fear ropes into a halo
& I am headless.

Churchless I believe
no psalm praises life

fuller than a chorus of wrens
on a spring morning

verses scribbled at night
are my prayer.

At dusk the sun paints
graffiti on the darkening sky

& the hope of turning to
stardust settles.

Breeze stirs leaves
& on a windowsill

a bluebird folds its wings.

Remote Control

Coronavirus sneaks in
a breath at a time. Schools & businesses
close. Streets, airports, parks
eerie with emptiness but for the discarded
blue masks on pavement & grass
& the constant flashing of ambulance lights.

Frost burns the blooms off azaleas.

I text my children. They work remotely.
My son offers a one-word reply: Okay.
My daughter responds with a photo
of a solitary roll of toilet paper & an emoji
with furrowed eyebrows. *Scary,* she texts,
How long will the lockdown last?

At night, rain plays cymbals on copper sills.

In Louisville, undercover police force
their way into an apartment where a 26-year-old
Breonna sleeps. They fire ten rounds of shots. After the death
of George Floyd, protests against police intensify.
CNN reports the virus has mutated 14 times.

Forsythias are flames against the cobalt sky.

Lines to food banks & vaccine sites
are miles long. In unused stadiums,
soldiers assist with vaccine distribution.
Police in full riot gear guard town halls
& streets. For hours, children stare at screens.

A pair of house wrens flaps & squeals. Are they courting
or arguing?

It is now a year after my husband & I developed
a new routine: we watch news while binging on coffee,
we walk around the lake & sit on the deck.
After dinner, we follow the updates
on fatalities—the numbers are rising.

It is two months since I threw a remote
control at him. It hit the bridge of his nose.

I Miss Mask Mandates

Behind blue masks

teeth under construction
grinding curses

glossless lips pulling
the mouth corners down

stayed in disguise—

what we saw was the eyes
dimmed with common fears.

We don't wear masks anymore.

No one smiles or makes eye contact
as if offended

by this act of nudity—the ugliness
of the last two years

etched on our faces.

Inertia

i cannot say i didn't notice
his blank face & unfocused eyes

a TV screen blinking on mute
a silenced iPhone next to a chilled

bottle—each metallic snap
an entry way into ferric frenzy

every honey-colored mouthful
a portal into hazy inertia

Mirage

it wouldn't unclinch—
this sepia feeling fueled by daily dismays

a despair crawling close to the skin
red ferrous rage

& like a crazy optical phenomenon
intimacy becomes celibacy

marriage—a mirage.

the god particle

a loud thud disrupts
my morning meditation
on the Higgs boson—

those yellow & green waves
that smashed in blackness & keep
the universe on the verge.

i gasp when on a sunlit window
i see a shadow—
an imprint of tiny feathers

v-shaped wings rising
above a round belly & small head
twisted at an angle—

what an impact it must have been
that hurled its lifeless body
yards away from the sky's reflection!

bluebirds bring a message
of hope but this one
mistook glass for air

my home for heaven.

We go on

because we learn
        to live with lies

because we are not the only ones

because a blue jay's round eyes
        prove something wise & ancient

because blackberry hope

because ice
        stops the bleeding

because the wound wouldn't heal

because disbelief

because honeyed   warmth
        in someone's eyes

our bodies splitting
        the water   the wood

because for months a dark room

because terror remains

that the pain of leaving doesn't pass
        to our children & their children

because icebergs
                trapped light

a waning moon against the steel sky

because at the end
        we go on   as memories

With Gratitude

I am grateful to Finishing Line Press for their continuous endorsement of my poetry.

My sincere gratitude to teachers & writers whose instructions & wisdom helped to craft many poems included in this chapbook: Chris Beam, Martha Witt, Timothy Liu, John Parras, Christopher Salerno, Maria Mazziotti Gillan, & Dorianne Laux.

Special thanks to friends & poets: Anna Appel, Mary Crosby, Jeanne Fleming, Karen Lee Ramos, & Val Schermerhorn for their insights, advice, & laughter during our get-togethers.

Appreciation to poets: George Bilgere, Mary Makofske, Mihaela Moscaliuc, Michael Waters, and Emily Sernaker, for taking time to read and thoughtfully comment on this collection.

My gratitude to my husband, Peter, for his support, and to my children, Sebastian, Kristian, & Karina, for their love & kindness.

Much love to Karinka for letting me borrow her powerful painting *Women in Society* for this book's cover, & to Sebastian for creating the cover's design.

Born and raised in Poland, **Edytta Wojnar** received her MFA in Professional and Creative Writing from William Paterson University.

The author of poetry collections *Dandelions in Third Space*, published by Stephen F. Austin State University Press, and chapbooks *Here and There* and *Stories Her Hands Tell*, published by Finishing Line Press, Wojnar received a 2025 Individual Artist Finalist award from the NJ State Council on the Arts.

Her work, nominated for the Pushcart Prize and Best of the Net, has appeared in *The American Journal of Poetry, Cagibi, CALYX, Glassworks, Lips, Lumina, Paterson Literary Review, SurVision, The Stillwater Review,* and elsewhere.

You can find her on Instagram *@edyttaanna*.

www.ingramcontent.com/pod-product-compliance
Lightning Source LLC
Chambersburg PA
CBHW022059080426
42734CB00009B/1423